S0-BZN-898

Susan L. Friesen
nfriesen@impulse.net
423 N. Lucas Dr.
Santa Maria, CA 93454

On the land, in sky or sea,
meet God's creatures
from A to Z

Animal Alphabet

MARY RICE HOPKINS

AND CHUCK INGOLIA

ILLUSTRATIONS BY

WENDY FRANCISCO

CROSSWAY BOOKS • WHEATON, ILLINOIS
A DIVISION OF GOOD NEWS PUBLISHERS

DEDICATION

FROM THE AUTHOR
To Cody Hutchins, a very special friend
who has inspired so many.

FROM THE ARTIST
To my encouraging and artistic mom,
Cathlene Hofheimer.

ANIMAL ALPHABET

Copyright © 1997 by Mary Rice Hopkins

Published by Crossway Books
a division of Good News Publishers
1300 Crescent Street
Wheaton, Illinois 60187

Art Direction/Design: Cindy Kiple

First printing, 1997

Printed in United States of America

ISBN 0-89107-968-8

05	04	03	02	01	00	99	98	97
15	14	13	12	11	10	9 8	7	6 5	4	3 2	1

A MESSAGE TO PARENTS

When it comes to God's creation, one of my favorite Psalms says it best: "Oh, Lord, what a VARIETY you have made! And in wisdom you have made them all! The earth is full of your riches" (Psalm 104:24).

As a mother of two, I am always looking for new ways to teach my children while exploring God's vast creation. In this book we've interwoven God's Word with a variety of His creatures and the lyrics to the *Animal Alphabet* song. Interestingly enough, the idea for the song came while I was with my stylist, Chuck Ingolia, at the hair salon. Isn't God full of fun surprises?

It has been a joy to work again with my good friend Wendy Francisco, whose artwork and talent I am so grateful for. I'm sure that you and your children will enjoy exploring the animals that Wendy has so beautifully illustrated on these pages and that God has so wonderfully created.

It is my hope that through the "featured creatures" in this book, your kids will see for themselves how much God delights in His marvelous creation. Have fun!

A is for anteater

...Believe in the Lord Jesus, and you will be saved...

ACTS 16:31

B

is

for

a

bat

...all things were created by him and for him.

COLOSSIANS 1:16

C is for a camel with a hump upon his back.

Come, let us bow down in worship, let us kneel before the Lord our Maker.

PSALM 95:6

Do not be afraid, for I am with you ...

GENESIS 26:24

D is for a duck

and elephant starts with E

Every good
and perfect gift is
from above . . .

JAMES 1:17

...for it is good to sing praises unto our God...

PSALM 147:1 KJV

F is for flamingo and they always bend a knee.

G is for gorilla

. . . *Go into all the world and preach the good news to all creation.*

MARK 16:15

He has made everything beautiful in its time.

ECCLESIASTES 3:11

H
is
for
a
horse

don't forget iguanas, they start with **I** of course.

In the beginning God created the heavens and the earth.

GENESIS 1:1

J is for a jellyfish

Jesus said,
"Let the little children
come to me . . ."

MATTHEW 19:14

and **K** is a kangaroo

Know that the Lord is God. It is he who made us …

PSALM 100:3

*Love
is patient, love
is kind.*

1 CORINTHIANS 13:4

L is for a leopard, they've got a spot or two.

M

is

for

a

monkey

*My help comes
from the Lord, the Maker
of heaven and earth.*

PSALM 121:2

...Never will I leave you; never will I forsake you.

HEBREWS 13:5

N is for a nightingale

O is for orangutan who doesn't have a tail.

O Lord, our Lord, how majestic is your name in all the earth!

PSALM 8:1

Praise be to the Lord ... who made heaven and earth!

2 CHRONICLES 2:12

P is for a platypus

Q is for a quail

. . . *quiet words of the wise are more to be heeded than the shouts of a ruler of fools.*

ECCLESIASTES 9:17

R

is for
a rabbit
whose
hopping
never fails.

*Remember your
Creator in the days
of your youth ...*
ECCLESIASTES 12:1

S
is for
a big
snake

*Sing to
the Lord with
thanksgiving...*

PSALM 147:7

The heavens declare the glory of God; the skies proclaim the work of his hands.

PSALM 19:1

tiger
starts
with

T

U is for an urchin who lives beneath the sea.

Understanding is a fountain of life to those who have it ...

PROVERBS 16:22

V is for a viper

...victory rests with the Lord.

PROVERBS 21:31

W
for
wolf is next

Wait for the Lord;
be strong and take heart
and wait for the Lord.

PSALM 27:14

eXalt the LORD
our God and worship at
his footstool; he is holy.

PSALM 99:5

and the Latin
word for swordfish
"xiphias" with
an X

Y

is for
a yak

You may ask me
for anything in my
name, and I will do it.

JOHN 14:14

...zealous always for the fear of the Lord.

PROVERBS 23:17

and zebra starts with

Z

This is the Animal
Alphabet Song
It's for you,
from me!

Animal Alphabet
Animal Alphabet
I'm a gonna sing
I'm a gonna sing

The
Animal Alphabet!

ANIMAL ALPHABET

MODERATELY

WORDS & MUSIC BY MARY RICE HOPKINS & CHUCK INGOLIA

Chorus

An-i-mal Al-pha-bet (clap clap) An-i-mal Al-pha-bet (clap clap)

I'm a-gon-na sing I'm a-gon-na sing The an-i-mal Al-pha-bet (clap clap) *fine*

1st Verse

A is for ant-eat-er__ B is for a bat C is for a cam-el With a

hump up-on his back D is for a duck And el-e-phant starts with

E F is for fla-min-go And they al-ways bend a knee__

SECOND VERSE

G is for gorilla
H is for a horse
don't forget iguanas,
they start with I, of course.

J is for a jellyfish
and K is a kangaroo
L is for a leopard,
they've got a spot or two.

THIRD VERSE

M is for a monkey
N is for a nightingale
O is for orangutan
who doesn't have a tail.

P is for a platypus
Q is for a quail
R is for a rabbit
whose hopping never fails.

FOURTH VERSE

S is for a big snake
tiger starts with T
U is for an urchin
who lives beneath the sea.

V is for a viper
for W wolf is next
and the Latin word for swordfish
"xiphias" with an X.

Last Verse

Y is for a yak And ze-bra starts with Z

This is the an-i-mal al-pha-bet song It's for you from me

to Chorus last time

Besides *Animal Alphabet*, Mary Rice Hopkins has also published the popular children's book *Hip, Hip, Hip, Hippopotamus*. However, Mary is best known for her creative ministry in children's music. Mary writes and performs songs with a special message for children of all ages. Her songs help kids and adults alike understand who God is and how much He loves them, put into practice the principles of sharing and caring, and realize how valuable they are in the eyes of their Creator.

If you would like more information about Mary's cassettes, CDs, videos or songbooks you can call 1-800-274-8674.

To receive information about booking an appearance with Mary, call 1-818-790-5805.

Or write her at any of the addresses below:

BIG STEPS 4U

P.O. Box 362, Montrose, CA 91021   E-mail: BigSteps@aol.com   Website: http://www.maryricehopkins.com